This Story Has Gone Wrong

Level 11 – Lime

Helpful Hints for Reading at Home

The graphemes (written letters) and phonemes (units of sound) used throughout this series are aligned with Letters and Sounds. This offers a consistent approach to learning whether reading at home or in the classroom.

HERE ARE SOME COMMON WORDS THAT YOUR CHILD MIGHT FIND TRICKY:

water	where	would	know	thought	through	couldn't
laughed	eyes	once	we're	school	can't	our

TOP TIPS FOR HELPING YOUR CHILD TO READ:

- Encourage your child to read aloud as well as silently to themselves.
- Allow your child time to absorb the text and make comments.
- Ask simple questions about the text to assess understanding.
- Encourage your child to clarify the meaning of new vocabulary.

This book focuses on developing independence, fluency and comprehension. It is a lime level 11 book band.

This Story Has Gone Wrong

Written by
John Wood

Illustrated by
Irene Renon

Chapter One

The Beginning

What are you doing here? Yes you, the one reading this book. What are YOU doing here, on page 5? No, no, no, this isn't like other books you have read. In this book you don't start at the start.

My name is Gubbs, and I am a wizard in this story. You must be the Reader. I've been waiting for you. Don't worry, I won't tell anyone that you came here first. That will be our secret.

Just do what I tell you to, do you hear? In this book, you are meant to start on page 44. Go on, turn to page 44 and start reading there.

Go.

Now.

This room is steamy. It is full of pots. Each pot holds a droopy, faded flower. All the flowers are dying for some reason.

In the middle of the room is a big bath. It is hard to see anything through the steam. But it looks like there are lots of rubber ducks in the water. And there is someone in the bath. It is Gubbs! He is taking a bath.

What are you doing here, Reader?! Can't you see I'm in the bath? This is so embarrassing. Don't tell anyone about my rubber ducks!

Please!

I told you to go to page 44. Now, off you go!

Chapter Three
All Aboard

The train speeds through forests, mountains and cities.

The train is full of swans. There are swans pushing trolleys full of chocolate and sweets. There are swans making honking sounds into telephones. Even the driver is a swan.

There are lots of boys and girls on the train too. They shout and scream excitedly as the swans chase them about.

I hope the swans are keeping the children safe. Where are all the mums and dads? Now that Anna has gone, everything is a mess, and nobody knows what they are doing.

Is that swan pointing to something on page 10? Let's turn over and find out what is going on.

The train is going through the mountains. There are lots of cliffs and gaps, but most of them have bridges.

But something is wrong. Up ahead, the bridge has been destroyed! It is cracked and broken, and there is a big gap. The train is going to fall off the cliff! The children scream and the swans honk.

Oh no, look! It is Gubbs, and he has blown up the bridge. We are all in danger! We need to save all the children and swans.

Wait! What if we skip the next page and JUMP to page 14? That way we can jump the gap. Quick, Reader! Jump to page 14!

The swan driver presses the brakes, and there is a screeching sound as the train tries to stop. But it is too late. The front of the train slips over the edge. It hangs there, swaying in the wind. Girls, boys and swans are all holding on, their feet dangling in the air.

The driver swan honks in fear.

The trolley of chocolate and sweets slides out of the train and falls down the cliff. Now the children are screaming.

It is a long way down…

ARGH! Help! Why did you turn to this page, Reader? I'm scared of heights!

I can't hold on much longer. My fingers are slipping. Turn to page 14 and skip this gap!

You did it! It worked!

The train is on the other side of the cliff. The children and the swans are all safe. You saved all of them! There is lots of happy honking from the swans.

"Thank you," say the children.

Well done, Reader!

But we can't rest. Gubbs must be somewhere nearby, and we need to find him as soon as we can. There is a farm just over the hill. I will go and look there.

Do you see that tall tower in the distance? Go to that tower. That would be the perfect place for Gubbs to hide. The tower is on page 18. Go and explore it!

Deep underground there is a cave. In the cave, there is a graveyard. In the graveyard, there is a lake. At the bottom of the lake there is a box. And inside the box is a girl. Is this the person you've been looking for...?

Sorry, I am not Anna. My name is Chen.

Don't worry, Reader. Nobody trapped me here. I just came down here to get some peace and quiet!

This story is a mess now. There are honking swans, trumpets, pigs and screaming children everywhere. This used to be a nice story where you started at the start and finished on the last page. But now it is ruined.

I hate it. I'm staying in this box.

Chapter Four

Messing With Magic

The tower stretches into the sky like a long, bony finger. It is the kind of tower that a wizard would live in and practise spells. There are giant webs outside. Is it a trap?

Inside, the tower smells of old books and burnt wood. There is dust everywhere, and the stairs creak when stepped on. The tower is very old. It doesn't look like anybody has lived here in a very long time.

There are hundreds and hundreds of steps leading to the top of the tower. Along the walls are paintings of witches, wizards, knights and swans.

Was that a creak at the top of the tower? Is someone here? Turn over to the next page...

CRASH! BANG! THUMP!

Someone is falling down the stairs! It is a very long way to fall. After hundreds of crashes, bangs and thumps, they land on the ground. A big cloud of dust rises slowly into the air.

Ouch! Sorry, did I frighten you? I'm always falling down those stairs.

My name is Wilbur. I am the wizard who lives in this tower. I used to teach Gubbs magic. Gubbs is a very powerful wizard now, and he can cast all sorts of spells. I think he is trying to cast a spell to take over this book. But I'm not sure exactly what spell it is.

Let's go and sit in those chairs on page 22. Turn the page and follow me.

I'm afraid Gubbs isn't here. It is just me in this tower. I wish I could help you. Everyone in this book misses Anna very much. But Eld misses her more than anyone. Look, can you see the painting of Anna? She looks very brave, doesn't she?

Wait, who is that? There is someone over there.

Sorry to barge in. I'm here to talk to the Reader.

Hello, Reader! I'm one of the children from the train. Do you remember me? I have a message to give to you. It is from Eld. Eld wants you to meet her on page 26. I think she has found Gubbs. Hurry!

"Can you hear that?" says the small boy.
"No," says the tall girl.
"Someone is calling for help!" says the boy.
"I can hear them! They are saying HELP HELP HELP!"

The girl listens carefully. She can't hear anything.
"We have to help them!" says the boy, running around. He looks in the garden. He looks in toilet. He looks in the fireplace.
"Where are you?" he yells.

The girl picks the boy up and sticks her finger in his ear. After a few seconds, she pulls out a tiny creature.
"Thank you!" says the creature, and flies away.

This was not part of the story. Why are you on this page, Reader?

Chapter Five

Surprise!

Ha! It is me, Gubbs! Did you miss me, Reader? Did you think you were going to meet Eld on this page? Well, surprise! I cast a spell on her and now she is trapped forever. The spell is so powerful, I am sure she will never break free. You will never see her again.

Soon I will take over the whole book with my magic spell. And then every page will be about me! Maybe then everyone will finally stop talking about Anna all the time. I never liked her...

Wait, what was that noise? It came from the next page. Let's turn over and see what it is...

It is the sound of footsteps. The footsteps get faster and faster, louder and louder, until...

There is a CRASH as a person bursts out of the bushes. It is Eld! She stands there, panting heavily. There are twigs in her hair. She must have run a long way. Eld is holding a giant hammer in her hands and she is ready for a fight.

Quick, Reader! Help Eld chase Gubbs. Don't let him get away!

What is this? Eld? How did you break free of my spell? This cannot be! I'm going to run away to page 32! I don't like the look of that hammer.

Chapter Two and a Half

This pig has stolen a wizard's hat and put it on. Now it is a magic pig! The pig can do anything he wants. Maybe he will fly to the town of trumpets. Maybe he will magic himself on the front cover of this book. Or maybe he will just roll about in the mud. Today is a great day for Mr Pig!

Someone has let that pig out!

Oh, hello, Reader. Are you looking for Anna? Me too. This story has gone so wrong now that she is gone. I was meant to be on a train with my son, but I missed it because of Gubbs and his spells.

I don't think Anna is here. Keep looking!

Aha! It was a trap! I tricked you!

I wanted you to come to this page. You see, Reader, this was all part of my plan.

At the start of this book I cast a spell. The spell would help me take over the whole story when the Reader gets to page 33. And now you are here!

No! We can't let Gubbs win. There must be something that we can do.

I know! What if we destroy this page number? That way, there won't be a page 33 in this book, and Gubbs' spell won't work. I'll crush the page number with a swing of my hammer!

Look, it is gone! Quick, let's chase Gubbs to the next page. Turn to page 34, Reader!

Chapter Six

Goodbye, Gubbs

We did it, Reader! We won. I have trapped Gubbs in his garden shed. He won't cause any problems in there.

You have been beaten, Gubbs. You've messed up the whole story, so tell us where Anna is so we can fix it.

I am Gubbs! I can't lose! It's not fair! Why does Anna get to be the star of the book? Why does she get to be the hero and I have to be a wizard that nobody cares about? I want the story to be all about me! Me, me, me!

You think you have won, but I will never tell you where Anna is.

Go and meet Eld on the next page, Reader.

Eld is sitting at the bottom of a tall tree. She turns away, but it is clear that she is crying. She is holding a picture of Anna. It looks just like the painting in the tower.

Eld wipes away tears with her sleeve and sniffs loudly.

We beat Gubbs, but I still don't know where Anna is. I miss her so much. I wish she was here.

Reader, I need you to promise me something. I need you to find Anna. Search through this whole book. Look on every page. Find her and make sure she is safe. And tell her...

... tell her that I love her.

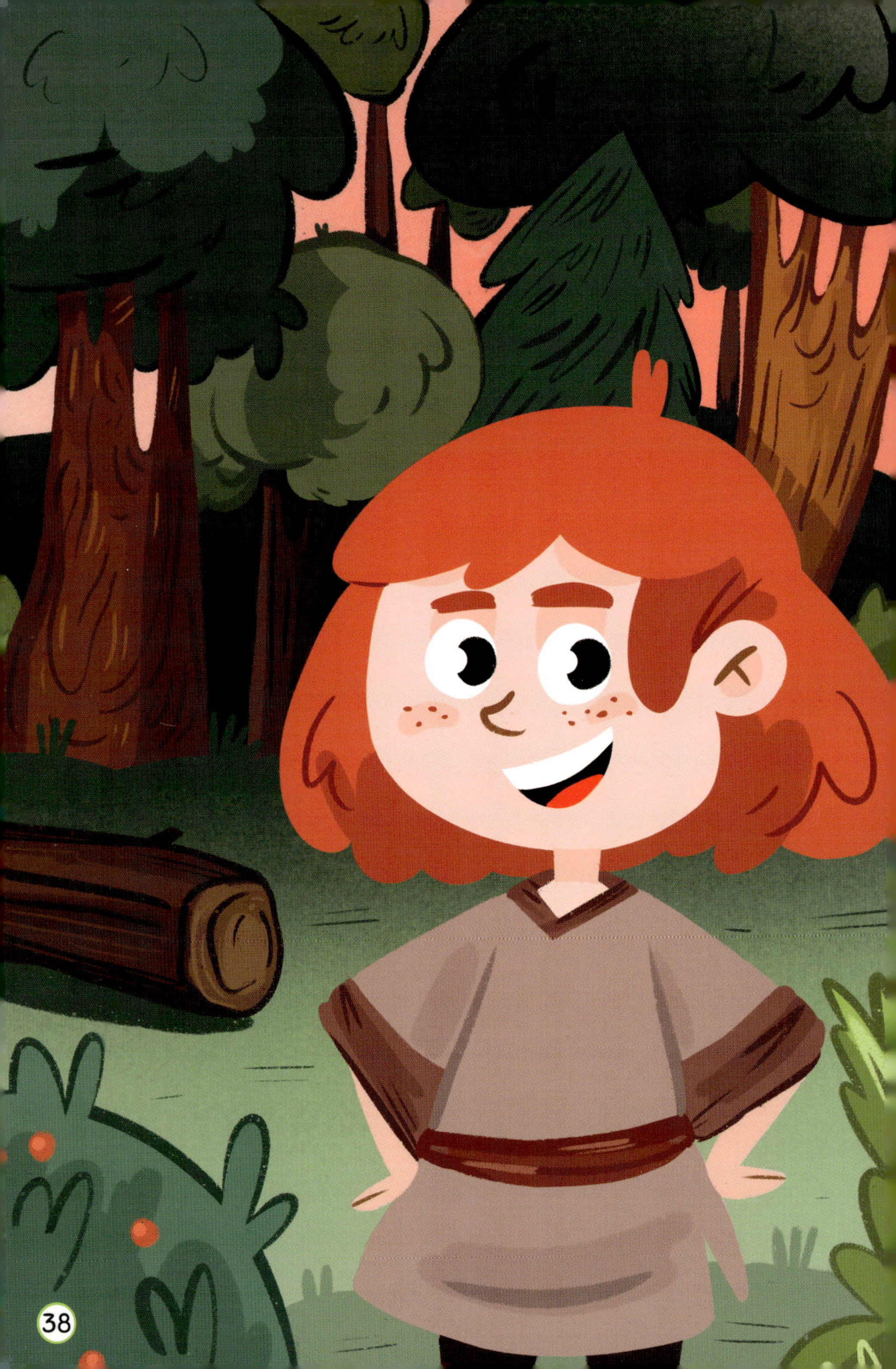

Chapter Two
The Beginning... Again

Listen carefully, Reader. This story should be about a brave knight named Anna. You should have met Anna on page 4, but Gubbs has messed everything up! He must be up to no good.

Let me tell you about Anna. Anna is brave and clever and beautiful. She has bright blue armour that sparkles in the sun. And she has a big sword to chop off monsters' heads. Don't worry, she only chops a monster's head off if it has been really, really bad. She is very kind most of the time.

Come on, let's go into the woods. It is just ahead, on page 40.

What did you think of Gubbs? I don't like him at all. Did you see all those dead flowers around him on page 4? How creepy.

People say Gubbs is a very powerful wizard. He is always casting spells, and it makes me very frightened. Magic is very powerful here, and it can do all sorts of things.

Gubbs must have captured Anna and hidden her in this book. Maybe if we find Gubbs, he will tell us where Anna is!

Look over there. There is a trail of dead flowers leading to the next page. Let's follow it and see if it leads to Gubbs.

Turn the page, Reader.

41

It is a town full of trumpets. There are people selling trumpets, and people buying trumpets. There are trumpets in the gardens and trumpets on the roofs. Each trumpet glimmers gold.

Look, that man has a trumpet for a nose. Maybe he knows where Gubbs is.

Hello! Are you talking about the ugly man with the dead flowers? Yes, I've seen him.

He went to page 8. Page 8 is very far away, at the other end of this book! You will never catch him in time.

Don't worry! Do you see that train over there? It is going to page 8 and it is very fast. It is leaving soon, so you better get on it now.

Take the train to page 8.

This pig is so dirty. How do you get so dirty, Mr Pig? And you are so SMELLY. You smell like a big pile of –

Oh, hello! You must be the Reader! Wait, why are you on page 45 already? Who sent you here?

Gubbs did? Oh no! This isn't meant to happen at all! This is very bad!

My name is Eld. It is my job to clean the pigs. But this story isn't about me, and it isn't about Gubbs.

Look, Reader, we are running out of words. This is the last page of the story – there is no room to explain everything to you. Quick, meet me by the woods on page 39.

This Story Has Gone Wrong

1) What happens to flowers when Gubbs is near?

2) Who lived in the wizard tower?

3) What animals were on the train?

    a) Swans
    b) Elephants
    c) Bears

4) What did you really think of Gubbs? Don't worry, he can't hear us on this page.

5) Have you found Anna yet? Hurry!

BookLife PUBLISHING

BookLife Readers

©2021 **BookLife Publishing Ltd.**
King's Lynn, Norfolk PE30 4LS

ISBN 978-1-83927-413-8

All rights reserved. Printed in Malaysia.
A catalogue record for this book is available from the British Library.

This Story Has Gone Wrong
Written by John Wood
Illustrated by Irene Renon

An Introduction to BookLife Readers...

Our Readers have been specifically created in line with the London Institute of Education's approach to book banding and are phonetically decodable and ordered to support each phase of Letters and Sounds.

Each book has been created to provide the best possible reading and learning experience. Our aim is to share our love of books with children, providing both emerging readers and prolific page-turners with beautiful books that are guaranteed to provoke interest and learning, regardless of ability.

BOOK BAND GRADED using the Institute of Education's approach to levelling.

PHONETICALLY DECODABLE supporting each phase of Letters and Sounds.

EXERCISES AND QUESTIONS to offer reinforcement and to ascertain comprehension.

BEAUTIFULLY ILLUSTRATED to inspire and provoke engagement, providing a variety of styles for the reader to enjoy whilst reading through the series.

AUTHOR INSIGHT:
JOHN WOOD

An incredibly creative and talented author, John Wood has written about 60 books for BookLife Publishing. Born in Warwickshire, he graduated with a BA in English Literature and English Language from De Montfort University. During his studies, he learned about literature, styles of language, linguistic relativism, and psycholinguistics, which is the study of the effects of language on the brain. Thanks to his learnings, John successfully uses words that captivate and resonate with children and that will be sure to make them retain information. His stories are entertaining, memorable, and extremely fun to read.

This book focuses on developing independence, fluency and comprehension. It is a lime level 11 book band.

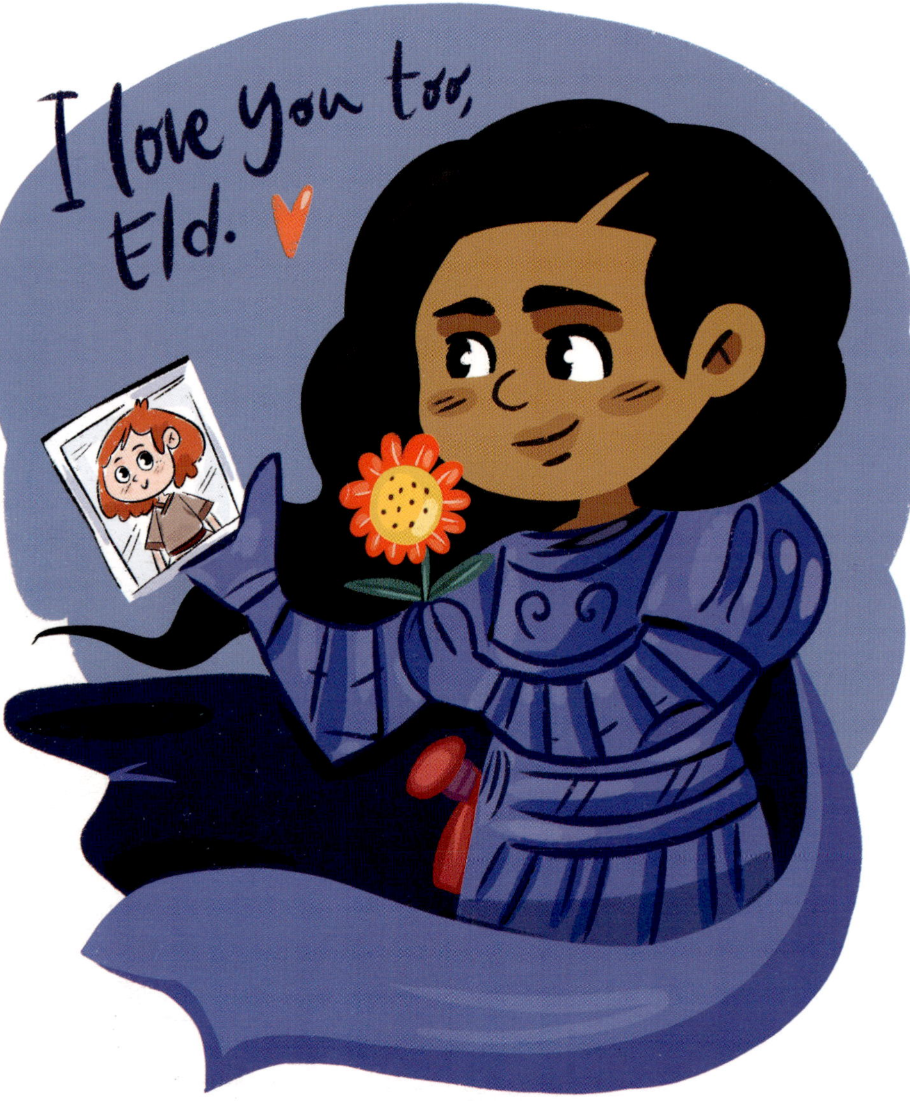
I love you too, Eld.